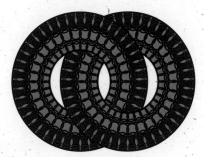

# The Red Canoe

## LOVE IN ITS MAKING

*a verse memoir*

# The Red Canoe

### LOVE IN ITS MAKING

*a verse memoir*

*by*

## Joan Cusack Handler

## CavanKerry ◊ Press LTD.

CavanKerry Press Ltd.
Fort Lee, New Jersey
www.cavankerrypress.org

Library of Congress Cataloging-in-Publication Data

Handler, Joan Cusack, 1941-
The Red canoe : love in it's making : a verse memoir / Joan Cusack Handler. -- 1st ed.
p. cm.
ISBN-13: 978-1-933880-08-2
ISBN-10: 1-933880-08-2
1.  Marriage--Poetry.  I. Title.

PS3608.A7R43 2008
811'.6--dc22

2008020544

Cover art by Oscar Astromujoff © 2008,
Author photograph by Matthew Licari,
Cover and book design by Peter Cusack

First Edition 2008, Printed in the United States of America

CavanKerry Press is proud to publish the works
of established poets of merit and distinction.

CavanKerry Press is grateful for the support it
receives from the New Jersey State Council on the Arts.

*for Alan, always.*

With grateful acknowledgement to the editors of the following journals
in which these poems first appeared:

§

*Boston Review*: "Homes"

*Confrontation*: "At Thirteen: Kneeling Beside My Father"

*Diner*: "Lessons", "Wounds"

*Journal of New Jersey Poets*: "The Marriage", "Like Good Mothers", "Grievances"

*Seattle Review*: "Quiet Bed"

*Southern Humanities Review*: "Fences", "Triangle"

*The New York Times*: "The Red Canoe"

*Westview*: "Husbands", "I'm Never Sure What to Expect from a Marriage"

*Worcester Review*: "Lost"

*Zone 3:* "Instruments, Weapons, Tools", "The Score"

§

Many many thanks to my editors, Molly Peacock and Baron Wormser, to designer Peter Cusack and the
staff of CavanKerry Press, and to the insightful readers of this manuscript: Raphael Campo, Teresa Carson,
Rita Charon M.D. Ph.D., Karen Chase, Florenz Eisman, Alan Handler, Robi Ludwig PsyD., and Carol Sny-
der whose comments, I believe, have made this a stronger book.

And more thanks and love than he can imagine to Alan for freeing me to tell and finally publish the story of
his life and mine.

# Contents

*I'd have to go back through all the stories to get to our marriage.*

# The Red Canoe

## LOVE IN ITS MAKING

*a verse memoir*

COUPLES


It's Jamaica. Philip, our boatman, guides us quietly down Orangetown River.
Just the two of us
                    and the frail parched carcass
                                    of Mylanta
                            lays herself down
                        on her lanky mate
                and he holds.
                                    Beside them, Mongrel thrust
                                        greedy fingers into
                                                the water.
                                I picture them
                            clawing the black
                        earth beneath—
it's an unfinished story,
                    but finished really—we know
                what happens in the dark,
            how we cling to each other
        sometimes harshly....


                                    Water Coconut, the giant fern,  big as
we are,
            keeps watch over the beach.
                        *We have 105 kinds of*
                        *fern in Jamaica*, Philip says,
                    another bouquet of Mylanta,
                beside it a dogwood, an almond, this river ripe
                                        with life....


    We all know the reason I love you—the bigness, the complexity of
roots;
            Dolphinhead Mountain's in view now
                            and we're smack in the middle of a Seurat painting.


                                    Lago Trip turn gleeful faces
            to the sun—

this river laying itself bare—
                a burned out cave,

                                more Mongrel, shameless in their rush for –
what is it?
        Food?
                The home inside a lover's chest?


                                Lacy limbs of Mylanta,
                Queen of Earth,
                        speckled with white buds;
                                *It blooms*, Philip says,
                *but only at night.*


        A goat looks out from a fleshy mountain
                        of green,
                grunts, nudges her
                mate safe
                        in the arc of
                                her limbs;
                                the wide grey breast of
                                        mountain makes it's way back to the sea.
All around us cottonwood throw thin fingers clapping into the sky.

# 1

*Legacy*

# FIRST LANGUAGE

Someone left a message                 on Joelle's machine
       saying     her husband was dead.
                                       It's true.
                                       That's how she found out.

For months, she said,        she  lived
                            with
                            an
                            Ice
                            pick
                            jam-
                            med
                            inher
                            chest.

                                I try to imagine the phone call &
                                    ice pick       but

cannot.
      My chest  won't  heave
            with revulsion.
      My head won't
snap back
     in desperate refusal.
          This frightens me.
               Has Anger built its monument
                      so
                      deep
                      inside
                      my
                      chest

that even an assault
like the threat of
       my own husband's death does not move me?

                    I reassure myself:

even anger is   Sha-
                tter
                -ed
         by     Fear
which                      Nature provides
                                        to protect us from
THREAT.


                              *Fear*     then, is
                         our first
                            language:

                                                    the mother
                                                    tongue.

              Mother always
              watching.

                         *Ah*,  so I am not frightened
              because
                         there *is* no threat here:

                              the old house
                              my husband
                              built   inside
                              my chest *is*
                              there. *He* is
                              t  h  e  r  e
                              smoking his pipe
                              in grandfather's chair.
                              & the fireplace &stove
                              &two mugs by the bed:
                              A  l  l   t  h  i  s
                                 L  i  f  e
                                    he's
                                    made

inside
me.
I keep it
safe, deep
beneath
the anger
where the
L I G H T is.

# EVERYONE HAD THEIR OWN RADIO

                                        Mornings he rose to his own alarm,
dressed, ate Cheerios & locked the door behind him
                                        with the key his Mom pinned to his schoolbag.


    Later,
the familiar sound of radio voices
                    welcomed him     when he let himself in
                                to the huge dark
                                        apartment
            after school.
                        Eating peanut butter & jelly on Wonder Bread
                        at the white enamel table in the kitchen,
                        he switched stations     searching for
            *Superman*  or
                *Batman*,
                        finally settling on
            *The Lone Ranger*.

                                        But somedays
                his radio wasn't enough,
                        so he'd walk  the six blocks up Broadway
                                    to his father's office
                                    & sit in the Waiting Room
                doing his math or looking at pictures
                        in *National Geographic*.
                                Once he found comic books
                stuffed  in the side of a black vinyl chair:
                                        *Roy Rogers,*
        *Gene Autry & Billy the Kid.*

                                        At home,
        he hid them
        under his
        bed.
                But, *There's no time for comics in <u>this</u> house*, his mother said.

Other days, he walked in the opposite direction
                              to The Yorkshire Apartments managed by his mother.
He'd throw a Spaulding
      high
      against
    the chipped
      brick
      building          trying to block out      her complaints to the Super
              about  tenants, mortgages  & housing violations.
                                             In the  background,
      her radio:    static competing with sirens   &  alarms,  the scary sound of
                              *The Six O'Clock News.*


              She seemed so unhappy there,
                                    he never knew why
          when asked where she lived,
                        she answered *The Yorkshire.*


                                    *Who'll do it if I don't?* she'd snap
                                          when he asked why
                    she had to work Sundays.
                    Even Dad stayed home Sundays.


          Saturdays at four,
                    he cleared his desk & father & son took the bus downtown
                              to Grant's on 42nd Street
                              for hotdogs,  then a movie.
                    They didn't say much —
                              baseball scores, what movies
                                          were playing.
              But this was a
            safer silence
                        than he felt with his mother
                    (quieter somehow).


                                    *<u>My</u> office <u>never</u> closes,*
            she'd bark, when he asked
                        if she could come too;

*Who'll be there if a pipe breaks?*
*The super has weekends off.*


Conversations like these   made him
              feel hot all over
          especially his face &   real sick  in the pit of his stomach
                    like he did    when he
                          bought bad hot dogs
                                    from the peddler selling in the street.
          He wasn't sure why
                    wanting her home
                    said he was selfish,
                          ungrateful,
                                    but he knew
          he shouldn't ask for things;
                    what  she needed was quiet.

                                        When he was nine, she found him
    alone   in his room,
      radio      tuned
                to    *The Shadow Knows*    blankets pulled high over his face.
                                        He was tired,
                                        he insisted,
                                        not hungry.
          But she was not satisfied.
                              When she pulled back the covers,
                                        she found
                                        the raw red
                                        bruise
                                        under
                                        his eye.
By nine the next morning,  she'd enrolled him in a school          f   o   r   t   y      blocks
away.                          He took the bus,
                                came home
          just as the street lights clicked on.
                              The neighborhood  was changing,
                                so she didn't want him  playing

                                                        in the street.
        He taught himself chess
                        while the other kids played stickball.
For junior high, she sent him                               further away.
        Two trains & a bus
                                        to  Horace  Mann   way
        uptown.
                Came home                              l   o   n   g   after  d a r k.


                                        Summers he hoped for a job –
delivery boy for A&P or a paper route-
                                he heard on the radio *The News*
hired paper boys.  But his job was his studies, his mom said.
                                *Why do you think I work so hard*?
*You'll take a summer course - more math, maybe science.*
                                        He'd help the Super—
do odd jobs at the Yorkshire. *I didn't spend my life working    so you could*
*do menial work.*
                *Besides,    you're all thumbs.  Scholars always are*, she laughed.
He'd help in the office-  he could type now.
                        *You weren't cut out for this kind of work.*
*You'll be a doctor like your father.*


                                He found a station    that played   Blues,
        Bobby Short &  Saloon songs.              He might try piano….
She arranged for a classical teacher, applied for credit and bought a Baldwin Baby Grand.


        But he  never learned
                                        to feel comfortable
                        with the big black piano
                                that stood
                                                mute
                                & forbidding
                                        like a monument of
                        all
                                he  wanted   but
                                                learned to
                                        refuse.

He preferred    listening
                to playing

            &  fell asleep nights
    to Blues
            &  saloon songs
                        followed by
*The Inner Sanctum.*


In his house, everyone slept with the radio on.

## AT THIRTEEN: KNEELING BESIDE BY MY FATHER

Above us   the moon still lazy on its back:
the sun barely rising:  my father & I,
quiet as monks,        climb up the hill    to the  Poor Clare
Monastery.

Each move is  familiar:
like him, I
bow
my head,

finger rosaries in the pocket of my
overcoat,

press my Missal
into the warmth
under my arm.

I am preparing  my soul for the Holy Sacrifice of the Mass.

My father is  closer to God than to anyone.
Kneeling
beside him in the dark light of
6:10 Mass,    I am
like him:
happy,

holy,

willing to
give

everything,

grateful for the raw wood of the *prie dieu*,
the pebbles

from some other worshipper's shoes

biting into
my knees.

Still my
back
is
straight,

unyielding:          *I believe in God,*
                        *the Father*
                        *Almighty . . . .*     I am here
                                with Him
                            keeping pace.

At the Offertory,
        our prayer books
        give us permission to sit, but
                        my father & I
                            refuse to
                            give in

& our  knees
            bear
        the weight of
        our conviction.

                        At the altar,
                        the priest
                        prepares
                        the Eucharist:
                                    we are halfway there.

        The sun through the stained glass
                            windows,
                    lays lace patterns
                            on my fingers & I
        move them
                    in   delicate
                            configurations:
                                            red,
                                                    purple,
    blue,
                        studying        the way a
                    slight
                    shift
                                can change everything.

        Just a few more minutes:

back,
knees,
whole body
burning.          I close my eyes,
               picturing   the sun,
                    hot & r ed
on the horizon of the altar,     its s l o w
                    reverent assent,
                    like the Host
                    raised high
                    above
                    Monseigneur's
                    head.


                         But I cannot keep this
                              straight back
                                   & lean
                         my butt against the pew,
                    rub the pebbles from my knees.


Beside me he never moves,
          body in perfect
               prayer.
               It is always this way
                    with us — me & my father,
                         his holiness,
                         a profile
                         for me to fit into,
                         another
          shape to wear,
                    so at night I fall asleep,
          hands pointed upwards
          like the steeple of a church.
                    I practice
                    sacrifice:
                         rise each morning at 5 A.M.

       & give away
        my dessert
           after supper.


                    Still,

behind the grill & the veil,
  the Poor Clare Sisters,
    those other daughters
          I imagine he wished for,
     lift their pale voices
         perfectly    together.
             I strain, trying to
                catch one   human
                   forgetful,
            raising her face out of the dark
               blanket of the habit,
                   but
     I grow tired:  how much
        longer to Communion?
          Thank God he's genuflecting,
           now the blessing
         now we can finally
           leave   this   dark   place,
         go outside
to the Loud, Garish, Irreverent   B L A S T  of  SUN.

## INSTRUMENTS, WEAPONS, TOOLS

\*

Hands  claw the dirt
carving   w o m b s
for tomatoes,  beets,
geraniums &  roses.


Hands make everything grow.                    Large,
                                     sw o l l en,  they mash
                                        carrots with potatoes.

Mornings, they mold flour & butter
into smoking loaves then shovel coal
                                        & bank the fire.  Saturday nights,
                                  they rake tangles from long wet hair.
                      They struggle & keep secrets.

                              My mother's
          hands spank us:
     not the usual
            t h r a s hing, but
                   hammered blows
            to the back & shoulders:
                         her big belly heaving each time she
                                        clubs us     with all
       she knows  from
                   years on the farm breaking horses.
                   And  there isn't much difference,
                                     I imagine,
between beatings, us or the animals: her eyes,  wild with wet thrill.


          My mother is a soldier.

                         & her hands are soldiers:

brute, muscled,                    they do what they are told.

I am a soldier.


I do all I can to avoid combat.

*

Even my father's
great chiseled fists
cannot s a v e us.

                              Sacred, quiet,    they never
                      come   towards us to
                                  hurt or touch,  but like the

        golem,

                                        they  r i se
                                     al i ve
                                                to
                                     fix
                                          things:    glasses, toys,
                                  piano, toilet.

        They carve a desk for the youngest son  &   frames
                                                    for the
                                                    older
                                                    one's
                                                    paintings.

                      They build our house
                                        then pray over Sonny,
                                  who uses his brushes
                                            to paint

        Mom's red-rimmed eyes  &
                  hideous
                  knuckles,

                                        Father's  fingers,
                                     veined  & laced
                                        in his  lap or
        vanished    in his pocket.

                              & Sonny's weapons slap—              *his* brand:
                                  the WHACK

that Shames:

the fingers            between
        my                     breasts
                    like
                    knives
                    pinning
                    me,        then the prancing & shadow
boxing    & the rush of  staccato smacks   to my  cheeks.

*

Still mute,
like my father's,

my own limbs
do not rise to arm me.

They know they cannot .          Like
                                   limp
                                   ornaments
                                   dang
                                   -ling
                                   beside
                                        me,
                                       they
                                       wait
                                       for

instructions.

                    I am teaching them to touch.          See how
they s t r u g gle
    to stroke                my husband's chest
    & roam
        dark
         paths
      inside his
       clothes.

                    But it's not natural;          they are self-
                                                   conscious—
rushing back  under the blanket
        when *his*                     do not move to greet them.


                         Meanwhile,  his

        tools
        hold safe

　　　　　things:　　　books,　his pipe, the cat;　　they type,
press weights,　play chess,
　　　　　　　　　　　　piano…　　&
　　　　　　　　　　　　　　　are　content　to
hold each other
behind his back.

*

Watchful,   soon  resentful,     recalling
the familiar
language,          my own  c l u b s
                          stiffen,
                          protect
                          -ive, &                    w  h i r l  out
from their place      beside  me              to   S M A S H
                          my  husband's chest.

                     My mother's
                  heirs, my hands
                          aim
                          the
                          arrow
                          at the
                          center
                          of
                          my

            father's sacred heart.

# THE MARRIAGE

My husband's father sits across from me: same white shirt, faded
tie, waves of white silk hair.
                              "She was different when I met her," he says.
                              "Softer.
                                        Interested in things of the mind.


Thomashevsky picked her  to play a Gentile woman once.
She wouldn't do it.      She took no pleasure from her  Gentile looks.
Hated  the Mercedes, too.
                                        I finally sold it.


She & her brother                          owned a hotel in the Mountains.
                    A clever woman.
Common sense, I mean.
                              Understood  the Things of the World,
            like what goes on
                        between      man & woman.


                                        My sister Rose introduced us
when I went up there   to visit.
Went back a few more weekends,      &     we decided to get married.
                                        We went to City Hall.
                    She didn't want anyone there.


You have to understand,            I never really knew her very well.
Things  were different then.
                    You met, got married, worked hard to make a living,
                        sex once in a while.

Don't forget I was overseas
in medical school    for two years
after getting married.
She sent money every month.


First there was the War.    Then the Depression.    The hotel failed.
People had no money for food,                never mind  vacations.
But she still worked
to pay for my schooling.
She raised 5,000 dollars.


Money changed her.   It was my fault.
We had to support          my mother &
brothers & sisters          after my father died.
She blamed Rose
for   not taking over.
We stopped seeing my family
completely      after awhile.


I don't understand      what happens to her
when she gets  in
these moods.


A lot of hate.    She  can't help  it.
Never got over her cousins
lost  in the W a  r.      Now this  thing  with  you  two  getting married.
He didn't handle it right.    He knows how she feels.

Nobody's         closer
to a     woman
than her      son.

It's the Mother that counts.


                              That's why I wanted to see you.
We'll work it out  between the two of us. You'll take lessons, convert, have a
child . . . .          She'll come around.
                              Tell him that's what you want.


He'll go along with whatever you decide.

II

*Mothers and Their Sons*

# HYSTERECTOMY

## 1

*I'll have to take the uterus so I can hike up the bladder*, the surgeon says.
*Childbirth causes it. The head tears everything as it bursts through the canal.*

                                        "So childbirth is rape?" I sneer silently.

*The ovaries are up to you. You'd have to think about why you'd keep them.*
*They haven't done anything for years.*

                                        "Since giving me this small boy
in an Oakland A's Cap and Youth Gone Wild T Shirt!" I counter incensed.

                    *All they can give you now is cancer.*

2

I dream I jump off the table, take and place my ovaries in a silk lined box
and bury them as I would any other mother I depended on.

3

Hovering over me now, the surgeon's green head and chest. God knows why green is the color of cutting. Mask over my face hands up to no good push into me in another violation and I know he's a doctor but he's having his way with me in the dark behind the needle and I'm lying here like any good girl and he'll deliver me when he is finished left with less some part or heart torn out and tossed in some organ Potter's Field . . . .

Under the white lights, the knife poised precise. A thin line. Reds everywhere. Below me, tulips, crabapple, raspberry fists of azaleas. Faces of boys climbing trees in the playground. Cherry trees. Goddamned cherry trees. It won't wash off.

What is this season that turns the smooth edge of flowers into the sharp edge of knives?

5

Another sleepless dawn, walking in the woods listening for God. At my feet there's a green
parade of small things, a rusted silver oil can, the white of startled birch, a few daffodils out
where the earth dips down. Over there a huge rock like a great stone beast rises from the
leaves: some great God of life whose time is now and who delivers herself proudly out of
the belly of the earth, her wide mouth oozing green milk. I imagine a body pale and capable.
In the pocket of my jacket, the pills I forgot to take at breakfast: a splash  of blue, purple,
red for hot flashes, calcium, huge, white and maternal, the pale gold mirror of Vitamin E
to keep the skin from  dying, then the deep brandy megavite for everything else I'm missing.

6

But decay *is* what's happening to the body.

                                    Almost imperceptibly,  it begins,
the faint tugging along the sides of the mouth, cheeks falling in slack pouches—
my face, like hers, finally  letting  go, dropping back to the earth . . . .

7

Something happens inside when you wake to find
you've long since passed  the midway mark.

Still change is the slowest motion of all, so we hold on, insist, my husband and I take off our clothes, handle each other roughly . . . .

9

Around us now, walls of trees—some are old,  thick with listening; out there
by the road, a huge trunk, like a huge cupped hand, twisted and veined from
living on the corner between two shapes of wind . . . .

Other trees are sparse,
slight as a life at the bottom. What could be more fragile, more here for only
a moment, than the dogwood . . . so excited it sprouts shoots all the length of
its frail branches, white blossoms wide as a woman in childbirth, white faces
rushing with life using it up.

# GRATITUDE: SUNDAY AFTERNOON, EAST HAMPTON

                                                                    Deep in the belly of the wood,

our son calls, "Throw me some rope."
                                        He's making traps for the dogs
                                                    that threaten his cat.
                    Black crows   out back of the pool house
                            call out           and I close my eyes   as the m u r m u r of
            boys &
                        the m u s i c of crows take over the   w   o   o   d   s.

                                                            At the nursery this morning,
            we bought plum trees,
                            a juniper and a laurel. Have you noticed
                                            how the
                                                laur
                                                -el
                                            dips
                                        down,
            c r a w l s  a l o n g   the  ground to find the S U N
            like any life or body  that's known love?

                                                        Dusk alone at the beach-
                            my body, snake smoothe in the sand.
            I
          like it
         on my
        side,      the sun in late September.
     It steps
back     just far enough
                        for everything to rest:           the ocean
                                            settling down
before
  coming in Darker,   Wilder....

                            I move up the beach, pull myself up

on the dune grass &
          pee there in the open,          letting
                                          the breeze
                                          make its way
                                          through me,
                                          I answer
                                          as in
                                          Love-
                                          take
                                          everything
                                          in

                                                    then  lie  back.


Clouds
                    fan
                                        out

                                             like

                                                            frail

lace,
                    the hoot of an owl,
                                        a seaplane,

                                                            my son
scolding dogs in the distance?

                              Crickets.    Dinnertime.
                                                    & I have to leave this
               singing,
          this chanting and complaining, persistent c r e s c e n d O
          of crickets.

In the parking lot, a woman takes pictures

of a guy
in a little
red car,      his froth of hair, flaming as Maureen O'Hara's,

a cat
jumping
through
the sun roof

on one of those ridiculous afternoons
that people in love have,

which reminds me:

I have so many lives to account for.

The marrow.
Speaking from it.
Squeeze the salt from it, the wine
& the blood.

VERMONT   VACATION   TRIANGLE

My husband & son
fall asleep
holding
each
other.
I
dress;
I'll go
to dinner
alone.
We are
three
people
spending
se    pa    rate
time
together.
No.
We are two
distinct  units:
father  &  son,
& me,          alone.


*Why didn't you wake me?*
Alan says      getting out of bed.

At dinner    he asks
what is wrong.
"This is supposed to be   a family
vacation,
but
David shies away
from me,
smothers you

                                        with kisses
                                    ....I'm happy

for the two of you,
     but  I'd like
          to be
     part of
          that.


                              I know
               it's normal              but I'm
          just not ready . . .
                         *You're still important—You're the Mom.*
          *He's not going far*, he assures me.          *He'll be back.*

          .


                                        "How did you stand it
                              all those years
                         when it was
                    me
               at the
          center
               &
                    you
                         on the
                              sidelines?"
                                   *That's just the way it works.*


               *It's*
               *l i fe.  It's*
               *psychology.*
               *Freud was right.*

# MENTOR

                                        So many people
wake                    inside these marriage walls:
parents,
God,
nuns.
                        But the child
                        is holiest.
                        He is the balance:
                                                advocate
        for each                        side.

                        &they listen to him,
trusting
the way         his mind makes sense
                        of their world:
                                                sifting it,
        turning
it
    around
        then         returning it clarified.

                                                Too often
        children    rend their hearts
                        with
                        our wars.
                                        Blaming them-
                                                selves,
                        they claim our pain
as if that will
heal the breach.
                                Here though,
                        he knows it is not his
                                fault,
                                        so he speaks
                                        Openly,
        tells each              he understands.

& like Scribes in the Temple
s u r r o u n d i n g
that first Holy Child,
they L i s t e n
as he teaches them,
*MOM!*
*Let it go.  Back Off*!

Her husband
gratefully
e c h o e d.

Then     *DAD!  Say something!*
*. . . Don't just criticIze.*

And she hears

someone
in back
of the
curtain

repeating her lines.

# COVER

*Make room for me on this bed*! my husband insists  pushing my debris
from his side to mine.
*Jesus Christ*!   He continues, *You're buried there*!
Beside me,                          catalogues,

                                                       manuscript,
                philharmonic announcements
        eyeglasses,
telephone,

                                    coffee mug,
   spoon.
                Under the covers, trusted blue sweats.


                I rely on cover.


                *There are boys in this house!* my mother chastised me
as I rushedtothebathroom in my longflannelnightgown.
                  The only cover that counted to my mother
      was the blue quilted bathrobe that stood stiff
& prim as an over-sized lampshade.
                    (*In sixty years of marriage*,  she bragged,
       *your  father never saw me in less than a slip*.)

              & I learned  from my father
when he closed his prayerbook,  got up from his chair, stood in front of the tele-
vision winding the alarm clock.
               A couple on the screen
               had been kissing too long.
               His big body blocked the kiss.
             *It's time for the Rosary*, he would say.

Later, in his own dark corner,
surrounded by scapular, pipe,
teacup, Missal, *The Catholic News*
& books of Aquinas & Merton,

my father, by example, taught me
to cover
for love.

## HUSBANDS

Sometimes he is Christ reassuring me
that I am loved
but flawed.   & like Christ,
he has his biases.
But
unlike Christ who loves only
the soul,
requiring that  I  sacrifice
my body  &            all earthly pleasure
just as the caterpillar must
offer  itself
as prologue  &  gateway
to the fuller life of butterfly,

my husband doesn't attend to my soul.

He concentrates on the body
& what the body carries.            Since it's all we can know,
he says,
it's the only thing
we can count on. It must
then
provide its own reward.

## QUIET BED

Night inside this bed my body stretches stiff
along
the
edge,
                              out of reach unless
he moves over,            says  what he wants
by taking it.
                    This time, let *him* be the one to
let moving over        be his statement of need.

On other nights
                    I've
          curled
          my body
                    towards him,
                                        spread my palm
open on his chest  & I've liked that reaching.

          At shier times I hover
          close to the middle
                    where bodies touch          a  l most
                                        without intention,
          & when such touchinghappens,
                                        sometimes
I take  his hand.

                    But  now,   locked inside
my   own
darkroom,          I need  him   to  pull *me*
                                        bellytobelly.
Night after
night   I've waited        for  him  to  refuse
the distance.  Now  I'm
                              letting  this  quiet

settle  in                              between    us
'til I'm at home                              again
                    wanting              no one.

## PERHAPS IT STARTED

the moment she
pushed    you    out
from that warm
darkness
inside her,
insisted    you    into
a      world
where everything
is expected and
there are no such safe places.

And didn't it continue
when she got sick,
tore    you    off
the    breast  and
sent you away to her sister?

Wasn't it she then,
who taught you
never to slip inside a woman
without recalling  that you
must leave again?

Sometimes, you hesitate
as if that mouth between my legs
was only wide enough to
pushyouout
instead of    take you in;

but tonight, when you
move between my legs,
my hips lock
from some deeper separation
of my own

TRIANGLE

                                  Cleaning out closets, I find a plastic box marked

Ecstasy
Lingerie:  Satisfies Your  Desire   To  Be  Different.
                        Inside
            black fishnet bra & panties.

                                My mother-in-law gave these to me,
            she  pulled them out of a drawer         laughing,
                  "These will do *you* more good
                        than me."
I am pleased.  A mother's permission, perhaps—
                      she always insists  on the best
            for her son.

            But this is the set up,
                  the tease:    the place in the triangle
                      where the story switches:
I open the box,        take out
            bra & panties,   examine them—
                    size 8:
            bust 32,    hip 34;

At my slimmest,    I've
            never worn
      less
   than

14.

# RETREAT


*Your body just doesn't turn me on*, he cuts. In
side my face & throat: the red of ripping flesh-      the just inflicted wound
in that layer     beneath the surface.

Beside me, he's small & guilty: sorry as a child
 awed by the fire of
his invention &   how much  it's  managed to destroy.

My eyes want to close,
lids  push
downinto
sleep but

it's c o ld & dark in here &    my     B u t t    i s    H  U  G   E
under  these  covers:  S    P    R    A    W    L    E    D     a l l     o
ve r  the  b e  d,      it  Lumbers      from
side                                                        to side
slapping   the   sheets &   my face   with   its  Shame  & E x cess.

He

tenders a palm to my back   to warm & calm me,  but       knees
snap to
chest,
my spine
recoils

-a good mother.
Resuming her
earlier shape,
she locks me in her
huge fist:  another
safe womb

where I can hide.

# LIKE GOOD MOTHERS

She has no screens,
he says,  nothing to shield her
from the world.
He likes
screens.
His mother called him weak.
His father was weak.

But his face doesn't
tw
-ist
when he          says these things.
He continues to stir his coffee.

*It's best if you don't care so much,*
he says.

Like Good Mothers,
S C R E E N S,
shelter you from Hurt.

Just as the water
inside the womb   protects,
dulling
each wound,
S   c r e e n s
keep you safe inside.
& screens
build
homes:     rooms     where you can live
alone.

That way          you don't have to feel
too much
when
Anger is in the air

or   Love

or   Loss.

So . . .        since his parents' death,
their birthdays                  pass   with only
a tempered  grieving:
a  vague   unease   when his wife is
too  attentive.
Screens enjoy distance.

He finds it easier
when their son is there   to distract her.

Sometimes
though        she touches him
in that hungry way  his body
remembers.
Grateful        for her frantic tongue& hair,
he lies
back &
lets her
love him        as she wants to….

Then,
without warning, he is
walled again.
now,        w e e k s        for      him    to   touch  her,
& she will grow tired       &    angry.

Now she is deciding,
listening to him talk about screens        while he stirs his coffee, she
will not live
entombed
in stone.

Soon
she will    berate  him.
Sounding

more and more like his mother,       she will *S C R E A M*,
even     pound   his   chest,     " How can you say you love me?!"

But he will
     not hear her.
               He'll take hold of her
               wrists,        place     them
                         beside   her            & get out of bed.
                    *I refuse to let you hurt me,*
          he'll say.




                    Blocked,              exposed,
     masking                   shame,
                                   she will

hate him,
          blame   herself for choosing him   &   resolve again:   to protect herself
                              she *must* leave him.


               Safe again behind his screen,
          he will hold her then
                         & tell her
                                   he knows.

# THE PROBLEM

The problem is this:  she grows hungry between feedings
& keeps looking, waiting, growing impatient,
                                                            resentful. How can he hold back
with  something so natural?
                                    She tries lures,
                                                    disguises but is  unsuccessful.

She makes a litany
            of his
            loving
            phrases
            &repeats them
            reassuringly            when she feels alone—hoarding cards,  notes,
                                                                    rereading them
                                                            to feel happy.        But
                                    that is not enough
                                                She'll ask him casually over dinner,
                        "When you said  I was  Wonderful,
                                                    what did you mean?"  *Just that*,
                                                    he'll answer,    " I mean How
            am I
wonderful?            *Oh, I don't know.        I'm   not   good   at   Specifics;*
            *You just are.*            But  she  wants  more, keeps pushing, "But
you must know.            What were you  thinking of   when you said it?
It's so nice to hear."
                        *I don't know, Joan.  Isn't it enough that I said it?!*
                                    *Can't you  e  v  e  r    get     E n ough* ?!

## THE SCORE

                        The small animal leaps
                                inside her.
She makes the pesto he loves,
                                then bathes naked beside him     on the blue raft,
                                        fingers & tongue
                                                giddy,  inventive.
                *We could do this all day & tomorrow too*!
                                he says.


But now he dozes,
            passion sucked happily out of him
            content to stroke her gently
    in his own grateful language.
                                        But sex still beats inside her;
                                            the score is not even.
                                        She is waiting      for his fingers
                                                    to
                                                reach
                                            for her      thighs,
                                            hungry
                                                        for the
                                                raw     language
            her body speaks when it is finally claimed.


        *But I would have*!
    he insists.              "But W H E N?"  she s c r e a m s,   "I'm  <u>always</u>
waiting!"


                        So she gives g r e e d i ly
                then pulls back
                        when she recalls
                        her mother      smiling on her
                        empty plate      those nights
                            she gave      her share
                    of cake     to her    brothers.

Some losses are so old  they can never be made up for.

But  he too came from  a mother who took everything.
    & because he  refused her,     she injured him—
                                    not his body,
            just deep cuts            into the place
                    where  the person was
                            form
                            -ing.
                    The boy   he was
retreated.


                                    It became customary for him
                                        not to make contact
                                            with the world,
                    unlike
            the girl who became his wife,
        who never
    stopped  trying to please.
                                    Now when she touches him,
                                        it takes him time to feel
                                            the small repair.

            & once  loved,
                    he goes off
    alone            to that womb
                        inside
                        himself,
                                        this time happily alone.


            His room is warm now,
                        lush as a forest.
            He likes this terrain.
        He smiles at her
                                waiting there.


                                    So she screams

to bring him back.

She doesn't know it, but

that's what the screaming is for,

because once he is gone, she

cannot  retrieve him.

He'll look out at her

from his confused  wrinkled brow,

not understanding at all,

like a small child  looking  up  at an A d u l t,

overwhelmed  by what went wrong    after such a nice day . . .

the air inside him

still fresh & cool

& his own dark mother   nowhere in sight

until now

when she is  l e a ping out of his wife's mouth,

"This marriage will *break me* someday!"

## OUT THERE IT'S THE GREY AFTERNOON SKY

In here, it's his grey
afternoon eyes pursuing me stealthily, almost
sneakily into the bathroom: me, braless, ass barely
covered   in
stretch lace
bikinis.
The only way for him to look is covertly—
no one was ever direct in his childhood home.

But the dark,
lush country
of myvagina,
listening
a l ways
for this
lewd
dialect,

answers,
heating up,
faintly percussive.

Feigning business as usual,
he returns his gaze
undistracted    to his piano.
I close the door to the bathroom.
But later,
it's his grey evening eyes
stealing a look at my bare tits as I
strip at the foot of the bed—
intentionally
blaze´,
non
-committal,
feigning undressing
but    s t-
r ip
-ping,

                                        pretending not to notice    his
eyes clearing fast now,  hopelessly drawn in by   p a r a d ing tits, ass      hair
not missing a beat   of my staccato banter about paint chips       tile
        listelo,            brass & chrome faucets
                                before
                        s li n k ing
                into  night
                                gown
                                        &
                                        dropping
                                                exhausted
                                                    into bed.


                                Late
        in the grey 4 A.M. halflight,    I
                                reach for his ass cheeks,       squeeze him
            drowsily                            awake,
                        lick tits, sex hard,     senseless     'til he
                                rises
                            over me
                                &
                        there's nothing left
                        unclarified or
                        unarticulated
            in the steady persuasive nodding of his hips.

## I'M NEVER SURE WHAT TO EXPECT FROM A MARRIAGE

I want to be cherished.
Reassured.
I want to prefer sex to sleep.
I want  w o r d s
from an aggressive man:          one
right out there on the line
telling me what he wants
& needs.
But
my husband likes quiet.
I'm *relentless,*
he says   p a r a ding   endless  comment or   question— "What do you
think?   How do you feel?   We need couples therapy . . . ."
But he has nothing to say.

Silence frightens me.
Behind it  some
outrage or  wound
smolders  toohot
toform words.                                        My mother's taught me that.

& silence indicts:
it says  it is my fault.
So I
fill this Marriage  with  w    o      r    d s  that COVER
the S  I   L   E   N   C    E   W a r m   s a fe
Blankets that keep it  from   rising up on me
accusing.
But tonight
his silence
muzzlesme.

Words
s   c u rry
in

                    fren-
                              zied
              cir
                        - cles
                        in-
              side my
                        throat.              Louder & louder,
they repeat themselves,
                                    to me.

# LESSONS

                              Our son, David wants to hear
everything his teacher,
Isaac has to say
               about    his potential
                                   as a violinist: over &
over each word
            u ncovered
                    O p e n e d    up
                    like boxes
                    that hold
                    all articles
                    of      this
                    soul story.
                                          Together
we examine the contents:
                         context,
                                      nuance;
         gesture.
               A tough
               teacher      like Isaac
                                      so openly
      E n t h u s i a s t i c ?
                         *Did he say*
                                   *good, Mom,*
*or  Great?*
               *Was he smiling      or   serious?*

                                   My son talks like this—
he demonstrates
                    how each of us  needs  the
                              reassurance of
repetition
                    the story
                    re told,   re viewed  through each
possible

lens.

My husband likes facts.
Specifics:
who,      what,      when,      where.
He doesn't

see the
layers
of how
&why
tucked
away
in drawers

until David
encourages him to
look inside,
take thoughts      o  u  t,
turn
them
around.
Discover
the how
of
why.

GRIEVANCES


                                    A  swelling  constant in my throat now & a burning in my
chest as I make note of each new grievance—

                                              it seems we're helpless.


                        He must criticize; I must react.
                                              But he says I provoke him.
              He wouldn't be so critical                if I would be more rational
                              I need screens, he says,            distance.
     .                        *Think*, he admonishes.
                              *Emote less*.
                                              To him,  I'm an E X P L O S I O N: that
     torrent of      L        E        A        V        E        S
                              overtaking him  in today's November  W      I      N      D.
              I'm
              s c a t  t er.              I  ex a g g e r ate.
                              I'm rage, fire &  t e m pest.
                              I'm our bedroom:  a        c
                                                                  h
                                                            a
                                                      o
                                              s              of Christmas
                                              wrap,

                   f r en z I e d outfits
                              dang
                                - ling
                        from
              doors,              our      bed
                              smotheredin
                              books&papers
                              catalogues last
                              month'sphonebills.
                                              He likes boundaries.

              I'm t o  o m u c h
     dough  r I s I n  g  unattended in the oven,  dinner for twenty to celebrate each holiday;  I'm
              last  minute

everything:
postage,
haircuts,
gasoline & phone calls,
wine,
toilet paper, makeup&
dessert,
visits to the bank,
dentist  & colorist.

*I'm always cleaning up your mess!* he says.

I'm repetitious – turning life inside
then out;      I'm needy,
dependent &
insecure.          I'm endless crises,
tirades, dropped
bladder & hysterectomy . . . .

*I spend my life*, he complains, *taking care of you.*

*I know I love you, but I don't know if I can live with you.*

He's tired.
He needs
quiet.          Rest.

I'm intense, too analytical: "How do you feel?
What does that mean?  I'm at war with my body.
Maybe I'll go back into therapy."

*You're  moody,*
he says,

*depressed.*

He wants l i ght,    airy:      he wants
healthy:

an  Athlete,

maybe a  Bimbo,          nothing t o o

                                              intellectual.
He wants to laugh,
                              play tennis,          a little piano,
          get a suntan,
                                        make love
                                        with someone who
                                        isn't keeping score.

He wants  entertainment:
                    movies,
                              vacations.          He wants quiet.
    He wants
        peace.

              He wants to be bored.

# TAROT READING

| | | | |
|---|---|---|---|
| *Which* | *QUEEN* | *are* | *you?* |
| The | psychic | asks | spread- |
| ing | four | cards | in |
| front | of | me. | I |
| lean | towards | Wands | or |
| Cups, | but | she | in- |
| trudes, | *You're* | *not* | *Wands!* |
| *You're* | *Swords!* | *You* | *like* |
| *to* | *be* | *in* | *CHARGE!* |
| You | rule | every- | where |
| she | says, | in- | dict- |
| ing | me. | & | my |
| life | & | love | lines |
| are | long. | | |

.

*But I can't  understand why you're not celebrating that marriage*!

  she shrieks

    indignant      as if it were her own.

| | | | |
|---|---|---|---|
| & | each | card | comes |
| up | the | same, | *But* |
| *there* | *you* | *go* | *a-* |
| *gain —* | *there* | *are* | *three* |
| *LIFE* | *Cards* | *in* | *the* |
| *Tarot* | *&* | *you* | *come* |
| up | *with* | *Two* | *Big* |
| *Life* | cards | *say* | *it* |
| all | comes | *out* | *Okay* |
| *so* | what | *are* | *those* |
| swords | do- | *ing* | *there?* |

*&  All  that  ANGER . . . ?*

# APPETITES

I want *Sex*, all pervasive SEX;
      him ready at the door when I come home;
      jealousy & surprises, kinky sex games & negligees he shops for;
      whipped cream & brandy & his tongue licking my crotch;
      candles & crotchless panties & his cock rock hard;
I want to fuck in the movies, give blow jobs while he's driving or talking on the phone;
I want to kneel in the elevator licking his dick;
      him ripping my blouse off & sucking my tits;
      watching me in the shower, pissing in the toilet, making pesto at the stove.
I want to see his cock rise & fuck my tits.
I want to make movies; I want to get caught.
I want a month of Sundays & his, the first move.
I want *Affection*;
I want *Kisses*;
I want *Touch*;
I want *Words*.
I want him talking for hours about how he feels;
      saying he wants me 'til I get bored;
      crowding me with phone calls & *Please come home*;
      asking what I'm thinking, what I want & need;
      then listening to my answers for as long as it takes.
I want to talk about movies, clothes, friends & politics, love & machine guns,
      designing the bathroom & color schemes he likes.
I want him planning days off with me alone;
      shopping all day with me for clothes—sharing strong opinions about
      what looks best:  Do you like the black dress?  Maybe the red.
      Should I go short to show off my legs?
      You *do* still like them?  How about my tits?  Do you think I'm pretty?
I don't want power games or fights about money;
      I'd like him more generous, not caring if I work;
I want less cynicism; I'd like more hope;
I want him crooning *I love you*, stealing kisses in front of friends;
I want to be embarrassed hearing him brag
      of my latest achievement or how sexy I look;
I want him to apologize, stand corrected & say *Please*;

hoping I'll forgive him after a fight—trying little love notes & tempting desserts;
I want to tease him out of a mood.

     I HAVE *Love & Laughter, Admiration & Respect, Support, Dependability,*
          *Goodness & Intelligence & Twice Weekly Sex*;
     WE HAVE  two homes with all amenities, lavish vacations,
          money we can count on & the child we prayed for!

But I want to *Talk* about it; take it out & lay it on the table
     with wine & dinner  & stumble over words;
I want to spend time sculpting this marriage in words;
     reminisce about our meeting, the first night of the conference—
     when we first knew;
I want to talk about our wedding, getting pregnant, the night our son was born-
     him pushing me in a wheelchair when there were no cabs;
     how it feels to be a father; is our son all he needs?
I want to share dreams;
I want to talk about sex & fantasy; I want to plan it;
      invent new games;
I want to tease each other;
I want to know—does he miss his parents?  Are their birthdays sad?
     & Mother's Day & Father's Day?
     Is there an afterlife? Will we know each other?
     Are his parents here?
I want to know if there's something I do that makes him feel safe?
I want to talk about bedrock & home; envy, jealousy & greed.

     But I do.
     I talk about all of it;
     I talk; he listens.

I want him to respond,  initiate conversations, come up with new ideas;
I want to know how his mind works;
     how he gets from here to there;
I want him to want to talk with me to figure things out.
I want him to talk — about anything, everything, more than business & bills;
     how he thinks & feels;
TALK.  Please *Talk*.
I need to listen to you *talk talk talk*

# THE FATHER SPEAKS

                                        My father-in-law is missing his Wife.
Reassuring me how she had grown finally to like me,      he says,
                    "*That one's smart*,   she told me,
                    *she's good for him*."
                                        He recalls, laughing,
how she disliked me,   laughing more now,
                    what a   b   i   g   A   S   S   I had,

                                                        s

                                                        o

                                                        T

                                                        A

                                                        L

                                                        L.

        Him,  he never
        had problems,                    but then     women are
                                                different;
                    they sense things.



                                        A quiet man otherwise,
words
topple
unexpected     from my father-in-law's mouth,
                                just
                            fall
                                out
                    on the floor          or your lap;
                                            sometimes they land

on your face.

Like the time he says

simply, *You'll convert, have a child; she'll come around.*


He can do that:
solve problems, settle things.


Or the day we tell him

the results of the amneo:
our baby   is

a Boy;

he
stands
right up,
so out of character

there at the table—
just the four of us.     (A toast—   I imagine-
how  lovely!)

*No one*, he proclaims, *Will ever know     that my grandson's
mother is a Schiksa.   You'll convert.   You won't tell anyone.*

He is speaking
for the two of them,
his Duty          as Head of the Family.   I am *SCREAM*ing again;
beside me,  my husband  is  quiet.   **Speak**!   I
scream  silently,        Say, DAD ?!        How <u>DARE</u> You?!


Or that time, in the hospital,
he is failing,     just too tired, too lonely  for  Sylvia
to hold on
any longer.
He  sits up,  le f t a r m  o ut- st r e t c h ed,
index finger pointing—

God   instructing  Adam- *Stay together*!   *Don't split up*!

It's not as if we  talk of
    anything personal,
                                        he just knows things.

# THE RED CANOE

It's all just dry rot! the neighborhood bully
laughed as he tore off a chunk
                            of the tired red frame &
flung it                         over   the fence.
              No snap was left    in the wood,
              so it gave up easily.
                                Like our marriage,
          it needed care now    to keep it afloat.


                    But we kids
          patched it & kept it
              afloat with
          Love.


                              I even crossed the Sound in that canoe.
    Took my best friend Kit  who couldn't swim;
                                    that's how much I trusted it.
        Never once capsized  even  when  speedboats circled.
              We just held on  &  rode  the s w ells
          into the wake.
                      & in my Marriage—
          this time it was I  who was taken across:
          my husband so sure, I  so frightened—
                      even after  the Fire,  the deaths,
          the parade of illnesses,
              we held on.
                              Though  now
              we fall asleep     hugging pillows
          on opposite sides    of  the bed.


                              Suddenly,  I can't remember
    exactly  what   happened  to the  red canoe
                          & I'm wracking my  brain
              trying to recall    its demise
          or disappearance.   It's strange

               how, out of    nowhere
          you're retrieving    lost love & a kind of
             terror flashes    that provokes the search
         for that other piece    once taken so much
               for granted    that you no longer
turned around to watch or tend to it -


                                    like our marriage.
          Or the red canoe—
             we got it          after a great longing.
       Then we ate it alive:    dragging it up & down to the beach;
          one would finish,     the other would be waiting;
              never let it       rest, be quiet for awhile,
       until one day it wasn't   where I left it
when I turned around to use it.

III

*Fusion*

## OF WOMBS & SPINES

Like shepherds preparing the stable
I prepared my mind
Had you looked inside, you'd have
seen a bright light,
felt a bright heat
& you'd have seen

Sky.

You'd be alone
inside this most glorius place
like

Heaven                    might be. Though in
Heaven
there are  others.
Here      there was  room for
only
You.
I kept others at the gate
just as *Your* Mother did
tending the

manger
back then       when
clean    became holy—
the thinsheet,
the  donkey's ancient  blanket,
her own
frayed
shawl,
that
circle
of
sheep
guarding        your  cradle—

all
wombs  of sorts.

Like her  I let nothing interfere or
compete   with
You.
No smoke laced the air.          No dark perfume.
There was only   light.

Years   passed  without grumbling          no distraction or dreaming   no
lesser loves                    or expectations.

But  then,  as happens with
one who gives                         everything,
I grew tired.
I began wanting   something for myself.
Blaming You,
I convinced myself  I could no longer trust You
so I crowded you out
with long lists of Your sins.     Demanding      as a
colicky baby,
You could *never* be satisfied.

But that's
what my
husband
says
about *me*.
The   pain    at    the    base    of    my    spine
in   the   same   place   Yours   must   have   been
when   You   carried   Your   Cross.   I   am   now
the   same
height You
were when
*Your* back
gave  out.
So perhaps

it was *I* who
constructed
this Cross
inside me
&
my
t
w
i
s
t
e
d
spineis
the womb
that
continues
to        carry
Your
pain . . . .

Christ! Will you *forever* live inside me?!

# DARK

## 1

The goddess doesn't want to come down from the tree and reenter my body, Patasha says, kneading my ankles and legs which harbor a great darkness, she says. Only when the darkness lifts will the goddess return. I remind Patasha and the goddess of my smashed ankle that's never healed completely and swells to a huge bubble when it gets tired and aches unmercifully when the weather changes. And of course my legs harbor darkness, what with all the pressure that's on them—hauling this body without any help from ankle or spine which is now so unstable vertebrae slip out without the slightest provocation and finally the sciatica down the whole left side! Pain's drilling a hole in my brain.

2

*There's no medication or treatment that can control your back*, the neurologist said.
*Without Fusion, you'll need a wheelchair in less than ten years.*

But I told no one.

Four years later, I still haven't told Alan.

3

For some reason, I couldn't call from our bedroom, too scared and dark in there, the room
of my illness, all frail bones, broken body.

                                    But what do I say? So sorry for the kicking
and the screaming, the pounding on your chest…?  What's left is like hot wax off a candle,
my stiff rightness collapsed, melted really,  piled sore wound on sour wound, shaping a
sculpture of some real life brought once again to its knees.

4

Lately I've taken to praying again.

Though I call now only in crisis, I know You trust my intentions.

What I miss most about fierce faith is trusting my judgement.
When I believed, I was an instrument of Your design so my choices were really Yours.

Now that we're estranged, I let my doctor stand in for You, God.

With Alan on his right side.

# HANDS

## 1

52 years preparation for this one Olympian moment,  the back hauled in from its obstreperous wanderings. Sad to see it corralled with metal rods, posts, clips and screws but there's no other way. I choose the most impressive pedigree, a surgeon I can talk to,  one who takes my calls, invites my objections,  repeats himself,  clarifies all  phases of the  procedure and recuperation without  even  a hint  of hesitation or frustration,  who manages  somehow  to  be encouraging without making promises. Thank God, he laughs a lot and smiles generously;  the guy in X-ray says  he's worked  with  the  best of them and seen their patients pre and post surgery and no one can top him. *It's a new life*, his patients effusively offer. *You'll do things you never thought possible*. And <u>*yes, the pain is gone; there is no pain*</u>!

But I could die.

I could be paralyzed.

In the dark before surgery hands dance over me beckon me all around me hands green hands hands smeared with blood fingers like elongated legs find silent pockets hide things there take them away outside the sun cuts the ice on the Hudson and I struggle like those ice fists the current so hot rushing beneath "<u>Keep your hands off me</u>!" I scream (should have/wished I screamed) when the subway stranger shoves his fingers between my thighs so many people cannot see his mouth jeering behind me I tighten my thighs and vaginal lips try to inch away but he pushes further I must change the way I dress see how quick we are to blame ourselves and where do I go from black shirtwaist and blazer Blue hands green hands mottled red and white hands Christ' hammered palms the beggar's ancient palms In some far off city two men send huge cupped palms to grab my breasts broad daylight no gasp or scream no one looks business as usual least of all me what most astounds me is my silence the huge breath sucked into my chest stuck there gagging me leaving me voiceless the merry-go-round not stopping no one stopping shouting this is his privilege what is it that tells one man the world is his we're all out there as banquet what makes one take the other let him like those chocolates bitten into then returned teeth arcs and all to their little cups in their heart shaped box and speaking of teethmarks I never noticed the surgeon's fingers how could I have missed them All five doctors questioned researched diplomas voices ages manners scrutinized but I can't remember the hands the fingers the length of the fingers the palms and thumbs are they smoke –stained nails framed with oil and blood do they tremble when he gets anxious my son and I stop everything to tear at our cuticles when we get scared

# PATIENT

## 1

Drizzle of light, voices off to the right, computerized, no inflection voices, machines beeping tracking breath heartbeat mask over my mouth each breath knife stabs left lung Rib removed for bone graft tube in lung for drainage Light more steady harsh bright light machines beeping counting measure degrees of sickness each thin breath costs <u>I Cannot Breathe!</u> Inside my eyes, my frozen head flashes back and forth chest heating heaving <u>Take This Mask Off Me! I cannot breathe</u>! I scream voiceless into the abyss of my paralyzed mouth and body Out there beyond a voice . . . *How was your date last night*? "Not great," his partner laughs across my chest in full view of my dying. "Should have gone to the party". <u>Take this mask off me</u>! Dying now screaming inside my throat lung burning <u>I can't breathe! Please!</u> Eyes dart to call them fingers strain to drum the bed each breath lungs lunge on raw rib stub *Don't move, Mrs Handler*!  Handler misses Mrs. Handler beg my eyes to plead for me <u>Take this mask off me! I'm choking!</u> Each breath stabs . . . *Hold still*! *You'll pull out the tube*! *The mask has to stay. You must be patient*! "I'm sick of these blind dates anyway." <u>Lie still! Mrs. Handler</u> you'll just make it worse if you move. I hear you're seeing Helene on 4 East . . . .

## 2

"How much longer before you can give me the morphine? The pain's really bad."

*You'll have to wait 'til your doctor comes to write the orders.*

"Can't you call him?"

*He's not in his office.*

"But can't you page him? I don't know how long I can hold out."

*You'll just have to wait. He never goes home before seeing his surgical patients.*

*He'll be here before 5.*

"<u>But that's four hours from now</u>! <u>Won't you please page him</u>? He told me to call him if I needed <u>anything</u>! He said the morphine would start immediately."

*Well, he should have written the orders. I can't start the morphine without them. Rest now.*

*I have other patients to tend to.*

3

Stunned by the cold place we're trapped in, Alan takes over: calls the doctor, arranges for private duty nurses; he'll cover midnights but he must work and care for David and I can't be alone with these nurses. But nurses are women too. Have they forgotten what it is to be kind?

Something human inside them has died.

# AT HOME

## 1

I am a fool wrapped in a blue blanket looking for something to say.

Shadows and their awful doubts whisper at the window. My feet—cold. My head—filled with cotton. Alan plays scales on the piano; David plucks Bach; the cat dozes on the couch.

I'm more of an invalid than a wife or mother.

*It's time to return to work*, the doctor says. No, Doctor. I know this house: its turns and conveniences, its willingness to wait. I am safe within its walls, joints and bones. It offers itself undaunted, as safe map and glove. Like a flexible cast or loving parent, it assumes all care: keeps danger out, asks little of the back, no steps to climb, no unexpected turns, no cars or brutal collisions, no hideous laughter or pity. Extending its arms, it invites me to even give up my crutches and walk the hall from my room to the kitchen or my son's room alone. Alan brings a chair to the stove and together we fix meat sauce for supper. Nothing can happen to me here. No, Doctor. I won't go outside again until this back can carry me: bearing *her* share of my ordinary life: driving David to music or baseball or myself to the office or shopping for groceries or Christmas. But you need not be concerned; I'm not closed in here. I have windows: eight foot floor to ceiling windows invite other lives. Newspapers and TV tell me all I need to know.

# IN THE DREAM

He leaves *me* even after I'm well. But this time I'm philosophical: managing my life as if I had control. The dream continues: I put on my red silk jacket and black tights and go out to breakfast with Kit, my best friend from childhood. Red didn't go with my face, Kit would have said: Kit always wore brown. I never wore a color she approved of. But this time, Kit doesn't notice my colors. And I'm not even crying or aching, the burning in my back is gone and it really doesn't matter where we eat, but there's no place anywhere that has room except one that has down tufted sofas filled with couples and two straight oak benches like church pews left empty. We leave, knowing my back will not stand such punishment. Then we're on 50 St., a familiar corner, and Kit selects some familiar place: it's convenient I think to our office. We enter, go upstairs and are seated at the end of a long narrow table balanced at the edge of a large platform suspended several feet between floors in a huge empty room under renovation with no furniture, no curtains, no flowers or tablecloths only floor to ceiling windows that let in the cold

I am no longer sleeping!

IV

*Love Making*

ALL THERE IS


pain
started again
quietly,          taking its place
beside hunger, anger, sex, fatigue,
but soon it drowned out all other urges
S  H  R  I  E  K  i  n  g,  *K I L L!*  K I **L**  **L**!
& just as the  madman puts up the fight
to silence those voices—
so too my efforts—
arguments prayers mantras rushing— yet The Pain
of my   t
w
i
s
t
e
d
spine          becoming
a   l   l      there is,  s   m   e   a   r   s
i t s e l f   l i k e   f e c e   s
o v e r   e v e n   t   h   e
smallest detail
of my life.
Triggered perhaps
by just walking
or cooking dinner,
Pain
heatsup;   it
b
l
e
e
d
s
like new red shirts that

bleed into every other
color of laundry
I N V I N CIBLE
even to Nerve Blocks
cortizone injections, 3 times weekly Physical Therapy & Bed Rest—
p A I n 's R E D H a i R slapping my F a ce in the
W I N D.

I dream its raw map fades from
myface,
but nothing
quietsit, not Love,
not Sex, not those new
R e d Boots not Chocolate Bars from my husband, not even
my s o n's
pain free face.

# INDICTMENTS

Unaware of the weight of their indictment, people ask
in the elevator or cab,   *What did you do to yourself?*
"Broke my back," I bark.
There's a cruelty about us,
Catholics&
Freudians: believers in hidden causes,
a superiority
&unforgivingness that sneers
at our deepest selves.  So unlike
innocents  wounded by stray bullets, I am
to blame here
or rather that sly part of myself that caught me.

If I could be a child again,
I would offer this pain for the Souls in Purgatory,
as we did then, eagerly collecting sorrows & sufferings
like soda bottles which we redeemed for souls.
How many souls would these months be worth?
The nuns were never clear
about value. *Just be grateful for this suffering*,
they taught us;  it brought us
closer to heaven. If only
I could make righteous
these past months,  though without God
to anoint them,
these are times I'd rather throw away.

Just like poverty or my first failed marriage,
they are simple reminders of what life is.

## HOMES

I envy the nomad:

not tied to the ground—

my analyst's son,

born in New York,

opening a Bed & Breakfast

north of                                             San Franscisco.

Moving  f u r t h e r  &  f u r t h e r  r

f    r    o    m    h    o    m    e.

One's center must really be home.

For
me,
the
spine
is
home.

I have to  shore it  up again;
it's
still
topp
-ling.                                      .

Doctors keep
referring to
my tallness
&
gravity:
my
body's
in such a
rushto
findtthedirt.

(My head's too heavy & my chest . . .)

I want to leave my body.

Why not just let it
lie down,        soul

slip        out

quietly,

float    on    its
own
for                        awhile

find
some        new
home

or perhaps
become
its own.

## WOUNDS

My neighbor's goddamned
RED (!)canoe
like a raw wound
sits jeering on the thin shore.
Small jetties
seek adventure
in deeper water, while for me
rocks make walking
impossible.
Back pain is constant now.
A thin raw veil
covers all
like too much salt in food
leaves room
for no other taste.
Our marriage is the wound&
the salt
& this bed
is covered with its blood.

# THE BLOOD

*You'll need to arrange for 5 or 6 pints.   If you don't
have your own,*   this *surgeon says,
        you'll have to rely on the hospital supply.*


                        And isn't it just my luck
                        that I can't  give myself Blood—
        my veins,
          closeddown,
            toosmall.
                        An hour & a half in traffic, back   s c r *E* a m
i  n  g,  a half hour more of nurses roping my arms,
                                pushing
                                needles
                                  into
                                   my
                                veins,    trying to bully them
        into opening…

                        And it isn't as if they're adequate,  but just too
tired—  even ANGRY to give anymore….                *No.*       It's
                                simply another case of
                                a part of my body
                                seemingly intended
                                    for a child.
First my bladder, now my veins.

                How can anyone—let alone a six foot tall woman
                be expected  to get along on a girl's frail veins?


                                            Tell me, God,
                        what <u>were</u> You thinking,
            building me
            a body

casing   with A M A Z O N  P o s s i b i l i t y
thendwarfingitinside
witharrestedmachinery?

What should I trust—

the *FLYING* BUTTRESS of my Legs
or the fretwork of my veins?


&what could be Your point, God, making it  so hard


Your
bleeding
heart
thorned,
crowned,
in my mother's kitchen  for breakfast,   after school with
cookies,          over dinner        dishes?  You,
passive,                              forgiving,
nailed to
the Cross
in back
of Dad's
head at
supper,
over our
couch
in the
living
room,
over
my
girl-
hood
bed;
nights before sleep the six of us

on our knees
praying
the rosary,

kissing

                    the nailed
                    ankles
                                                    mimicking our father.


                    (Were my broken ankles  gifts too—
                    *my* share  of Your  Crucifixion?)


          And all this started with blood:
                                    not enough of it, the knife, too much of it,
          the nails, blood for surgery, Christ's blood, replacement blood, tainted  blood,
                                                    mydwarfedveins.


                    And doesn't it make sense that my blood's also rare
                    Not my husband or son,  not my sister, brother, nephews,
                             but my best friend & her husband
                             & if I'm lucky,  my typist.


                    & professional or not—I'll be desperate—
                    I'll accept  a pint from a patient.

                    Only four.


                    No more time.
                    No more veins.

# LOVE IN ITS MAKING

## 1

"But our marriage won't survive  another surgery,"
I insist.

"TWO SPINAL FUSIONS?!
How does this happen?

More months recuperation
& care -                  you're so tired.
We *both* are.
I just can't subject us to that."
*We should have done it*

*months ago*, he says     already assuming
his share of
burden.
"I can live with this
pain. It's been there all my life."
*You'll have a new life.*
"But what about last time?
& I
could
die."
*This guy's never lost anyone;*
*we heard the statistics!*

These talks are endless.
Each of us repeating our lines:
"I'm terrified of paralysis!"
*Less than one percent*
*nationally*

*& O'Leary not one.  They have*
*spinal cord monitors.*

<pre>
                              Vacillate
                     another
                 few months
                          seek fourth & fifth opinions;
             hear it
             again.    Beside me,  he asks
                              questions   I
     forget.


                                   "You'll have to handle everything:
                                        David,
                                        Work,
                                        Me.


                                   Alone."
                 I'll be fine.

                          We agree on time.
                 The dead of winter seems right.


             You'll want to enjoy Christmas
             & David's Bar Mitzvah.
                          You'll be up & around
             by the time Spring breaks.
                                   "There'll be months of no sex."
             We'll have time for that.


                          I schedule
                              the surgery for late February;
                 he books us on a cruise
                          the two weeks before.
</pre>

2

It's not the dark of night that frightens:
            the dark that
                    lays
                    down
                    gently
            on the trees,          &
                                never insists itself
into my mind.
        (Night        & the mind's light continues
                                        though darkest dark
sails me into sleep).
            Instead, it's the dark
                    at
                    the
                    end
                    of
                    the
                    needle  I fear,  that sends me
            where
                    the mind no longer is
            the mother I
                    depend on.
    I no longer
        know
        the
        shape
            of
            my
    own
        skin.          The day ends      when the light ends
            & I am taken from me.

            The mind
        is my only  beacon:        flashing  RED & *green*,

the mother who watches closely,
follows
every
move,     sends me signals—

when to wake, how to cross,
how to bless,
how to stop this knife from sl i pping.

3

                                                                      Barely wak-
    ing into the conflagration,
                                        I am raw wound;
                                                              I am ALIVE,
              awed,
                                even in this anesthetic stupor
          by this Satan
          that consumes me.

                              F l A ring  out  from my raging
                    center, it j E e rs,  s c  r E A M S its obscene
                    prayer  through  my ears, eyes, teeth,  even   hair
                    e              n          g          u          l          f          i          n               g
                    skin              air                          this                          room.

                                                                      What was once
                              my body  now is a smoldering log;
          no part of me                          has                                    escaped
                    the  *F        L        A              M              e        S.*

    Out there                              across  the wreckage:
    a  whisper
                        a faint
                        break    in the burning.

                                                  *How's my girl?*

        If    on ly I could  touch   him—        fingers, quiet as a child's,
                                                                      feather
                                                                      the tips of
                                                                          my fingers
                                                                      & nails:

            a  *douse*  of cool rain .

4


D a y s,    n i g h t s,
fInally
sleep's
cool
dark

AWAKE.
Returned:
all the way back    to            The  Awakening –
my will,
the only part of me to survive
the F i re,    in   one   A M A  Z O N I ON      E ff o rt
strugg-
ling
up
through
the flames
from the center   where I once lived,
insisting my eyes  O  p en (closed again)
to find him
next to me,
fingers
barely
touching          fingertips,        lips,
his
left arm
a  wide arc
on the pillow
above
me,
forming
the  womb
that encloses
me.

It's Mother.
That's what Marriage is
—knowing that
                you'resmall&
                inthewomb   again:
                                    because that's what
                this Pain is -
                it's having to
                be born again,
                knowing it'stime
                &    T    **H**
                                R
        *A*
            S   H   ing
        t  h  r  o  u  g  h
        t h e  c a n a  l.


But there's  this   Mother  surrounding you —
                in here     but
out there too—- coaxing you
                    whispering  in your ear
        that she'll be waiting:


            *Keep* fighting, he says,
            *just come  through*.

5

He is my Voice
&   Decision
                                        & (apart from the officious

metronome   of nurses),

                                        his is the only voice
                    in this room
                    where I lie
                    speechless
                    in my profound
                    burning dumbness.

                                        Positions reversed—
                                        each of us   assumes this
        new role as if we've
        been born to it.

            From his place   beside me, he
                        gives instructions,
                    answers the phone,
                        questions doctors,  reads me my mail,  helps
    our son  with homework,  calls my parents,
                        explains    how I'm feeling to friends.

            When my condition is stabilized,
        he makes dinner with David
        and when he's asleep,
            drives to the hospital -
            with CD player &discs of
                                        Beethoven, Brahms &  Chopin—
            where he dismisses the night nurse  turns on
            the music & h o v e r s
                    over me
                    feeding me
                Ben & Jerry's  Cherry Garcia Frozen Yogurt   then

sleeps all night beside me on a cot designed for a child.  &
this rhythm  continues for almost th r e e w e eks.

I'm well taken care of,
I tell him;
You must be exhausted. You need a night off.
*I am fine*,
he assures me.
As my strength  inc r e a s e s,
I begin  speaking for myself.
He moves over
just enough.

6

Watching him clearing the bed
of my dinner tray,  filling the pitcher with fresh cool water, bringing my books,
placing them close,

I'm reminded:

He is Joseph all over again
caring for
Mary.


No one talks about Joseph


but it was he
who w a l ked  l o n g  hours in the cold night, lead the mule & the Family
to the  stable.


& who but Joseph built the manger?
His hands freezing cold,
brittle
but warmed
inside

by their perfect,
improbable task.

He made a home
where Mary could
do her Work.

& when it was time,

he delivered the child
& gave the mother her son.


That night was a night for humans
just as these nights have been—

no Gods or miracles    to erase
the necessary suffering.
That is what Christ was about:
human,  necessary

                              suffering.

          True, my need, this time,
                is not birth,
                                    & I'm not so important     in history
                      as  Mary,
    but days when I
        believe in God again,
                      I know He put Joseph &  Alan here
                        so Mary & I could finally feel safe.

7

That other night,
the night *our* son was born,
then too my husband was Joseph,
& just like the first one, he waited

& when I was ready, he picked up the reins & took me
where I needed him.

There were no taxis
& it was too far to walk.
But because he was Joseph,
he found a wheelchair
& gently helped me in.
Taking the handles,
he wheeled me
down First Avenue
to 70th
& as if time
spun itself
as far back
as he insisted,
traffic, obeying him,
settled down
& moved over, perhaps
even recalling
its own holy history
as donkeys & cattle,
the street a dirt path.
*Make way*,
his silence commanded.

There were no screeching horns,
just vehicles
prayerfully slowing
then stopping

as will happen
in the path of any sacred rite:
I'm frightened. *I am with you.*
I'm not ready. I won't make it.  *He's our baby.* I can't
do it. <u>*We* *will do it*</u>. I'm not ready *I am with you* Oh God! He's coming I can't
do this *Wewill do this*  Thy Will    be done.

8

Guiding me  out of the bed with tonIght's
rhythmic
           interpretation —        a staccatO,
mambo beat:
                    *Roll*        *O ver*              *legs down*          *pUsh*
*off*
          *Roll  O  ver*      *legs   Down*              *push*
                                                              *off,*
                                        he takes my right hand
                                                 in his,

& bracing
  my
  flaming
  back
  with
  tender
  muscled left arm,  leads me              VictOrious  &  L au ghing
      to the Bath Room.
                                            *Roll*
                                        *O*
                                          *ver,*
                                                *legs*
                                                    *down,*
*push*                            *off,*
  *roll over,*
              *legs down,*                  *pUsh*              *off* . . .

      Whatever  pain  there is  in these procedures,
                    he
                    MuS
                    -cLes              O   u   t   with
jOkes.
                                            &    joking    works –

      like Lamaze
          in child-

birth.      The Pain

circumvented:

                 outsmarted by the Competition - be it
                     jOkes  or b r e athing.


      My Pain  challenges  Him;
he takes it on
           as he does a chess match
               or game of  tennis,   all of  Life  in fact—


     poised,  prepared:
            giving it his Best Shot
                  but
turning on it
     laughing  when it
             esca l a t e s   into  m  O  r  e,
threatening to
     defeat him.
          Other than the two of us
            &David,    nothing is more
                  important
      than   his
        ability   to laugh
          at it.


           He tries to instruct me
        in this wisdom,    & I
    am grateful for his gift
though I'm too serious   to adopt it.

9

Somedays    I
come
at
life
side-
ways;
for instance,
not grasping fully
what our love is
until I          picture
our son grown up and away from me
nested
inalove
that re-
plicates
ours.          The mother
in me
who loves generously
wants this  for him,   & is happy.
But
the jealous lover who lives beside her in me
can't bear to
let him go
to this
greater love
who  now
w i l l  b e
his Center.
I understand then what our love is
when I feel my chest
c *R*  Ack
& I   long to
PULL   my son
back
from this

new   home
that  replaces me.

             I can't bear the assault
          of him loving another woman
             as I do my husband.

        But  that's what Marriage is:
            the child
            choosing
            a mother.

        It's the hot border where two
           soulsjoin.

    Somedays
        I  need
      to recall
that hospital room
          to remember—   *this* is what love is for.

V

*Home*

LOST

The first time I lost my husband
was 30 years ago,      the corner of Third & 59th—
10 minutes late, a signal, some-
thing went wrong, maybe traffic,  so unusual, he's always a few minutes early
t w e n t y   m I n u t e s   d r a g
t      o      w      a      r      d      s      a      n      h      o      u      r

my belly

drops

towards
the    pavement  al ready  t h e   G R I E V i ng  GR A-
SPing forG O D  F R a n   t  i c bargaining  promising  apologizing   a n
h          o          u          r          &        a        h        a        l        f
c o u l d n'  t   leave     that corner   for even a
moment  h e   m I g h t   f i n a l l y   G ET THERE      S E E   m E
gOne

leave

not expecting me
to have w a i t e d  s o    l  o    n    g  in the D a r k  D e c e m ber
c O l d.
But it's Christmas
so maybe he's not dead
but waiting
he too frantic on some other  corner  convinced  I too have
died   no other explanation for my failure to show    & it's
the thread of hope  that
that possibility offers
that pulls me    finally
from that
corner
into
the gutter                         straight
down
Third
into
the

                              lights
                               of
                            oncoming
                            traffic &
                            Christmas
                                        he'd surely see me
                            towards
                              any
                             other
                            possible
                             corner
                            between
                            here &
                            my office
                            on 50th
                               &

    HE *D I* d.

LIGHT


The night our son was born,
he cried.
He cried too
the day we married,
stood beside me
in our indoor garden—
our tree family:
Ficus,

R e f l e X a


Venus Aralia
H o v e ring
quelling parents
s p r e a d i n g their A r m s
for us,  joining hands, forming  the


C h u p p a h


—& spoke his vows,

I will.
I do.
Tears:

that other
amniotic                                blessing,
mother's
wet country.


He is able to do that;
after long stoic weeks,                    he stops
at some
life place
& Opens.

Without
warning—
     Tears.

      From some  fire life  inside
         himself,     one perfect letter
                                    I . . . .

      *I'm happy*

      *I love you.*

      *Yes.*

   No lead up,     no  embellishment  or clarification,
        Just
        fact—         like God,
           the judge's gavel,
              Dawn.

        That's what life with him is like:

l o n g    s t r e t c h e s    o f    q u i e t
then Cl i max-          Sun-
        rise outside
        the cloister
        door.
            Like the ruby necklace he gave me
one Christmas.
    No clues.
    No whispering or
      wrapping.

          Just red,
          amniotic
       LI G HT
       inside a
       bluegrey
       b  o  x.

## ACRES OF COMMON GROUND

His pipe
separated us.
It was that simple.
"I'm allergic to your pipe,"
I said.
*I'll smoke in the den*,
he answered.
& the fighting stopped,
each of us tending to
ourselves, free to
find our own
pleasures—him
chess, piano,
me books,
computer—
happily
stopping by
to say *Hello*, place a grateful
kiss
on lips
or shoulder.
"Twopiecesof
wetspaghetti,"
our couples therapist laughed.

Before,
left to our own devices,
we'd seldomseparate.
Rather than choosing what
each of us wanted,
we'd fake instead
the smallest piece
of common ground
&cramintheretogether,
content          at first

                                                            soon resentful
        —each tired of giving
                        in, not getting what we want,
                                                sick of the selfishness
                                                        of the other
                                        that defined that
                    tinypiece
                    ofcommon
                    ground.

# NOT QUITE HEALED

Finally
supported
by the
long
metal
rods,
inside
the
column,
the
marrow,
deep
inside
the
cord,
that
wombed
vein
that
brought
me
forth
b
e
n
t,
already
damaged
from my
mother:

one year today

since the  second
spinal
fusion

surgery &

I am not paralyzed.

I am whole.

I am healed

deep
beneath
the cuts
thediscs,
the bone,
held
obedient
& safe.

Still I
raise topics
like gauntlets: *My  Scoliosis was congenital!*
I rage
to my Mother &
her guilt rushes to Dr. Green. She
never missed a check-up; she
took us,  for the  slightest
sniffle…. But
I am not finished, *You blamed <u>me</u>*
*for not  s tanding*
*t*
*r*
*a*
*i*
*g*
*h*
*t!*
Relentless,
I  shoot questions:
searing,
brutal   as her
hands once *were—How could you*

*treat it so lightly?    Why didn't you  dO something?*
　　"We trusted our doctors . . ." she whimpers
finally leveled.


　　　　　　　　　　& when will I be finished
blaming her too
　　　　　　　　　for my　rushed resolutions?
If she had just
　　　　　　　given me　r o o m,　let me
　　　　　　　　　　　　　m o v e
　　　　　　　inside my life,
　　　　　　　　　　　　　　without
fear of risking
　　　　　　　her love. . . .


　　　　　　　　　　A mother myself,
I now know
　　　　　　there wasn't even
　　　　　　　　　　the slighest possibility
that she would not love me.
　　　　　　　　　　Yet still I
　　　　　　　　　find it hard
to look her straight in the eye.
　　　　　　　　　　Across from
me, now, no longer God's
　　　　　　warden,　　she is  frail,
　　　　　　　　　　　almost
frightened,
her lined forehead pleading forgiveness. . . .


　　　　　　　　　　True,
　　　　　　　the road to  H e a-
l i n g . . . might  have  been
shortened—
　　　　　　Mother  is the First Healer:
　　　　　　　her Milk,　her
　　　　words,
　　　　　　eyes,　　hands,　　E l i **xir**

or

POI SON

       (more likely
         mixed).

                  But it takes so

l o n g  to know

              the   difference.

& she's 84 .

        As    I      leave    her,
        A r t h   ri    tic    hands
        like    rust   -ed   gar-
        den    tools,

     ca
     -pa
     -ble

        of    lit   -tle   more
        now than   ra k   ing
        her   I-    ron   col-
        ored
        hair,

             r e ach up
              to
           touch
          my cheek.

        It is
           I   now

who  l   o   o   m  H   U   G   E,
S t E   E   L   C o n S T R U C t e d,
even M   e    N   A   C i   n   g.

Driving home,

I remind myself,

there's solittletime.

# WALTZ

Mother, I call
but you still hurry off the phone to Court TV
disappointed,  disgusted really
with the latest verdict—
Dad in the kitchen baking bread.

Later, he might polish your fingernails,
drive you to K-Mart for pots or a kettle,
walk beside you with the wagon
talking too loud.

Some other day, you'll cut his hair,
empty the fridge of  carrots, potatoes,
leftover pot roast and make his
favorite soup.

Mother,  you are graceful dancers: him serving tea
and breakfast, you, lunch and dinner.
You haven't done dishes for years.

Afternoons,
he'll finish a desk for a grandson, then
pause in his corner with prayerbooks
and Thomas Merton;
across from him,  you'll read
large print Agatha Christie
and watch Court TV with headphones
until 6 o'clock,
when you'll switch channels to
Sr. Maria and
together, you'll say the Rosary—
Dad, straight-backed  on his knees, you stretched out on your recliner.

Mother, imagine now, a phone call—
a son or daughter—

"Is there anything
                    you need?  Milk?  Tea?
          The steps shoveled?"

     *We're fine*, you will say,

*We have everything we need.*

# CENTER

                                    All my life
I've avoided the m I d dle:
                    the w a t e r e d
                                    d     o     w     n
        version,  all cOlors
                        muted –
                        middle of the road,
                        midlife,
                        even middle of my
                        body.
                                        But here
                    in the center of this
                            marriage,
        it's that place                          between us
            where          truth
                            sits:
                                        the third party
        in the room                 that hears him&
        hears me.
                        This   middle
                            collects
                                        all the gestures:
                    the   words
                        & not-
                        words.
                                        Perhaps we
                could      live
                            here:
                            lie
                            down,
                                r
                                o
                                l
                            l
                        into her

                        safe
                        arms;               she has room
for the two of us.
                        The middle    holds  our
        places, lets    his shade
                        &mine
                        mingle     together
without giving in              completely.

                        What safer
                        place
                        than
                        this—   where each
                                        of us
        gets    &    gives:
                                no side
                                left    unattended
        in the lap of    Good
                        Mother    we rushto.

# LITANY

Take for instance, our rush to bed as soon as we're alone in our Key West apartment:
the two of us
always grateful now, taking nothing for granted, not love, not sex,
not long walks (made possible by my rejuvenated practically enthusiastic back&spine),
not long lush silences,

not
talk, not words.

We have been spared—
I think it's safe to believe it—
connected
here at the center in sex as in birth,
reaching towards
the womb that
held our son.

Giving thanks
to my left 5th rib
from which eight new discs were formed,
Now I am
another Adam
making Eve possible.

Thanks too to  Flexible Titanium Rods,
for letting me bend to almost
touch my toes, pick up this cat,
throw my legs          high
to hug my
husband's back
d A nce

in
black
patent
high      heel
pumps

at the third birthday celebration of my reconstructed spine.

Don't forget
The fire quieting down along my spine enough to let me finally live my life:
Walking for hours the neighborhoods of Key West  with my husband,
Our son walking beside me now, no longer in front—clearing paths;
It's months since I've heard *Be careful, Mom, Careful,* his mantra
    'til he'd locked me  s a  f e l y  i nto m y  seat  belt;
I've turned in my *Handicapped* plates;
My car's no longer equipped with wheelchair, walker, crutches or cane;
I go days without Advil, Naprosyn, Tylenol or Percoset;
My first shower unattended was  Mother's Day, May 13th.
Despite threats of death, danger & paralysis, now I shop for hours for CDs & sneakers
    with David;
I ride my Lifecycle 40 minutes a day;
I drive for hours into the mountains listening to Mozart, Brahms &Joan Baez;
For Mom's 85th birthday; I'm cooking dinner for the family,
                    my back's letting me;
                        I want to;
I'm not scared anymore
                ( or almost)
                        though the faint ache under the wing bone this morning
reminds me:   Be respectful-
                    respectful as Alan was standing beside me through the
hysterectomy, fractured fused ankle, skin cancer treatment, clinical depression, cranky
spine, 2 spinal fusions!


It must have been so hard for him to talk to me,
but now that we  no longer hear our mothers' disapproving tones,
we have been spared to act the way a person does when they're at home &
living,  struggling,
                (somewhat spoiled).

Grateful,

the two of us,        finally

separate;

& believing it.

FENCES

Out    there,      grey

w e  a  t h ered  fence:
post   &
border
turn
in   every
direction
sculp
-ted
by
w   *i*    *n*   d.

No human
could  have  designed  that
alone:
like bodies weathered &
sh-
a
-ped
by
life.
Like  mine.
Like my tw-
ist
-ed
spine.

But no.
That  fence  is  not  me.
It is my husband.
He is fence.
I     am   w   *i n d.*
I am rough prairie,
the   *r u s h* ed   f i e l d   o f   f o r s y t h i a.

My        fence        s u r-        r o u n d s     m e,
gives      me        plA y        r oo m      but
keeps    me        from       *w an-*     *der*
-ing       too       far.        My       fence
is        arms.     I        L i ke      arms.
Arms     hold-     ing        me.       Late
-ly        it        greys,     soft      -ens

b
e
n
d
s
out     in places where I've teased it,
                   w e a thered & con v I nced it.

                       Other
places,
it
  p
    u
     s
      h
    e
 s
i n    onme   insisting,
               refusing     to  give in.

What were  once stiff young  posts,
        boards,     now     shift-   lean
                       in,
                           out,
       this way,
               that,
               accommodating my
rushedspeech,    *G  U  S  T*s,   w i l d   o ut-
         bursts   & 

                              d
                                a
                            n
                        ces  &   its need   for
boundaries.


        Lately, a l  l  boundaries  s o f t e n .  W   r     a     p
p  i  n      g          i t s e l    f        e   a     s-
    i    l     y          a  r  o  u     n        d    m    e
            I t
            w e a r s
            o    u    r


                            s


                            h


                            a


                            p


                            e


                        like
                            our
                        bed
                    clothes
                    after
                        love.

# HOME

## 1

All the time in the world—

hours                                on      a      Sunday     afternoon
         convincing
               a log          to        f  l  a re.

     The log
            takes        its        t   i   m   e     &&
will not be rushed.

Years since surgery:
                               in the absence of
pain, once my closest companion,
                    L O V E     S     *u*     *r*     G e
    s  through my life.

                       This morning, he wakes me stroking
      an arm
        then    reaching
           a  palm
           t o  cup
           a breast
                         make l o v e,
take a whirlpool,
                   make bacon & onion on bagel for
   David's breakfast....

                  Afternoon,
      he plays piano,

David violin,

I coax the fire..


We are family.

Family
                                            far
                                               from
my childhood.


Everything  eventually
gets said here.
                            Not as  often

as sometimes I'd like
or as  Ornately—                but definitely said.

I lOve you.
I'm scared.
One s
        l
        i
        p
         of the knife.


I am alive.

                            &  last night I told my husband
I finally feel safe.
Does he think it's safe to believe it?                I *so* want to believe it:
                    whole,
                    Mended.


                    *Less raw*,

                                                                    he says,
              he
         no longer   stand-in
   for   my mother,

                                    no more her
                                    agent  insisting
                                    if only I'd try
                                    harder,  I'd be good
                        enough . . .


                                                        Something about the surgeries—
                                        each of us
                                        carrying
                                        our share
   —how <u>never</u>  in  a l l  those months              did he tire of me,
              flinch,
              frown,
         roll an eye,
         snap at me,
                   he to whom criticism
                        came so naturally.          Suddenly,  he didn't seem to
                                                            disapprove of
                                                        anything about me!


                        How for myself    it was
                                          the single
                                          greatest
                                          drama
                                          in my life
                                            (next to childbirth)
              but No..                          G   r   e   a   t   e  r.
                   In      childbearing,          the decision
                        becomes final
                   months before birth;        once you  decide to
                        have the child,        you cannot turn back—
                             You *will*        give birth.

But in surgery
the control never leaves your mouth

until the anesthesia,    so
I could've said No! Don't do this! I could die! I could be crippled!


Instead
Isilencedmyself
insistingFusion
meant giVingmyspine
thesupportitneeded.


What it all comes down to is this:
I did it.
He stood                beside me but
I went
alone    into that blood dark.

When I get this far
down
to the bare bones of it,      I have all the time in the world.

2

The fire sends its final signal:

It's just not in the mood
to ignite.

I consider the power
of fire.

It makes its own
choices
&will not
be coaxed.

& I hear it  just as I hear
his wish for  silence,
as  simply a statement
of preference      like the fire's wish
to go its own way.

No longer deprived,

I drive to the beach,

hang out there lazy
like the grey
that holds  on

to the uterine sky.

Out there    the    h  o  r  i  z  o  n
effaces,
blue/
pearl /
white
grained

like ash,

t a kes m  o  r  e

r  o  o  m

How long it took
to  let him
love me
in his way.
So ready to attack,
claw,

discard   his quiet
offering:

it's not good enough,

never   enough. . . .

But the S  U  R  F
like my log,
has no trouble,

first it s p l a s h e s   s t r a i g h t   out
then it murmurs
to the side.

Two        gulls
scale the
water
as sun   breaks through.

Above,   grey
takes
turns

trading
places

with blue.

Now it's hard to tell  where the sky
ends&theOceanbegins,
so like that place we get to sometimes, where it's hard to

findthelinethat separates us,
soconnectednowbythefood:  the mother
                           feeding us,
                           the womb     rather than   the
                                        that   until lately    so often de-
                                                        railed  us -

l e a ving,

                                Yet  we
                                are
                                separate,   our  lives like trusted currents seeking

their own Karma
inside that bellied ocean.      Twinned
                                yet
                                separate,       like skin
                                        touching skin in the sunlight, we are sky & ocean.

                                                                I consider this

        safe womb
        I'm living in
        lately with
        my husband.

                        This marriage
                        womb is
                        possible.

                                        I consider the power
                                                of two.

## CavanKerry's Mission

Through publishing and programming, CavanKerry Press connects communities of writers with communities of readers. We publish poetry that reaches from the page to include the reader, by the finest new and established contemporary writers. Our programming brings our books and our poets to people where they live, cultivating new audiences and nourishing established ones.